THE MARKETER'S GUIDE TO LAW FIRMS

HOW TO BUILD BRIDGES BETWEEN FEE EARNERS AND FEE BURNERS IN YOUR FIRM

GENEVIEVE BURNETT | SALLY KING

ISBN: 978-1-925846-56-0
Published by Vivid Publishing
A division of Fontaine Publishing Group
P.O. Box 948, Fremantle
Western Australia 6959
www.vividpublishing.com.au

A catalogue record for this
book is available from the
NATIONAL
LIBRARY   National Library of Australia
OF AUSTRALIA

CONTENTS

FOREWORD

This book promises marketing professionals that it will help them:

- gain a better understanding of both law firms and lawyers
- think about their firm, their relationship with the lawyers they work with and how they can build better working relationships with them
- work with the lawyers in their firm to create marketing and business development campaigns that deliver concrete results.

The authors have delivered on these promises.

Sometimes when a client poses an insoluble problem, I have said 'I wish I had a magic button to push that would solve it for you'. For marketing professionals within law firms, this book is the 'magic button'.

This work by Genevieve and Sally exemplifies synergy. Together, they demonstrate a sophisticated understanding of both law firms and law firm marketing professionals and how the two might interact in a better world.

If being a marketing professional in a law firm were a game, then, reading this book would be called cheating because by reading it the marketing professional's chance of winning would rise meteorically.

Thank you, Genevieve and Sally, for providing this remarkable resource that I may share with all of the marketing professionals who seek guidance from me as to how they might enhance their credibility within their law firms.

Managing partners and their teams would also learn valuable lessons from this precise reflection of the current state of law firm leadership.

Two imperatives: buy this book and read it.

Gerald A Riskin
Founder
Edge International: a global consultancy to the legal profession

1: THE TROUBLE WITH LAW FIRM MARKETING

Dear Law Firm Marketer

We decided to write this book because, one day as we were talking over lunch, we found ourselves agreeing that there was a problem in the world of law firm marketing.

We had both noticed that most firms, especially smaller ones, were struggling to market themselves. The vast majority were getting themselves tangled in knots, especially as they desperately tried to adapt to the digital era.

We then talked to friends and colleagues working in the legal services industry – both marketers and lawyers. The vast majority agreed with us. There was something wrong with how most law firms marketed themselves, and the majority of firms were struggling to adjust to life in cyberspace. Even more importantly, most of them agreed there was a problem with the relationship between lawyers and marketers. Most lawyers rolled their eyes when we asked them about their relationship with the marketers in their firm. Interestingly, most marketers we spoke to had the same reaction when we asked them about their experiences of working with lawyers.

Next, we came across a survey ViewsHub conducted in 2017 that showed business development teams in professional services firms, including law firms, are ineffective and do not command the confidence of other employees. Business development people were ranked according to three criteria:

1. their ability to get things done
2. how technically good they were at their jobs
3. how responsive they were to other teams.

ViewsHub claims to have surveyed 50,000 employees working in nine sectors (communications, financial services, automotive, charities, food, media, technology, professional services and other) in the United Kingdom (UK). Professional services came out rock bottom. Business development teams in professional services firms were deemed slow to deliver results, under experienced and unresponsive to criticism.[1]

We are sure that both lawyers and marketers will agree this is a concern for law firms, which are all under increasing pressure from digital disruption and growing competition. The risk is that conventional firms will lose business to NewLaw firms, which leverage technology to poach clients from market incumbents, if these incumbents don't conquer the marketing and business development beast.

Then we looked at the marketing strategies law

firms employed, and how the problematic relationship between marketers and lawyers may be affecting their quality.

From what we could tell, most large national and international firms seemed to understand that they needed to conquer digital marketing in all its facets. We looked at the websites of the major international law firms. We soon discovered that, in most cases, these firms didn't seem to be marketing themselves in a way that enabled them to stand out from their competitors. Most large national and international law firm websites are remarkably similar and, in an attempt to master content marketing, many pump out endless articles that are nothing more than case notes. In short, the quality of publications coming out of these firms was uneven.

We also looked at the websites of mid-size and smaller firms. Although there were some notable exceptions, the majority of these firms didn't seem to grasp how they should be using the various digital marketing tools at their disposal; and when they did use them, the results were often sloppy, inconsistent and ill-conceived stabs in the dark that reaped few concrete rewards.

Interestingly, these patterns could be seen whether the law firms were located in the UK, the United States (US) or Australia.

The empirical data available for the Australasian legal market backs up these observations. In November 2015, the Australasian Legal Practice Management Association (ALPMA) and Julian Midwinter & Associates published a report based on a survey of 161 respondents in law firms across Australia and New Zealand. This research showed that nearly half (44%) of respondent firms did not have an overarching firm-wide marketing and business development plan in place. Of those firms without one, 80% were small and mid-size. Even more importantly, most of these firms were fighting static or declining revenues. Even more alarmingly, some were declining in size.[2]

Just as we were becoming a little nervous about whether it was possible for the relationship between lawyers and marketers to improve, we uncovered cases where marketing and business development teams very much admired their managing partners. In these firms, lawyers and marketers were working together to do all sorts of wonderful things. There were also stories of lawyers and marketers not only collaborating to come up with better models for marketing their legal services but building very profitable businesses in the process. Some marketers swore to us that they had a 'seat at the table', and others had become part of the senior management team. We also uncovered a few lawyers who were big fans of the marketers they worked with and who valued their contribution to the firm.

Soon, we uncovered quantitative data that indicates the situation is not quite as gloomy as the ViewsHub survey implied, and that the relationship between lawyers and marketers is currently undergoing a process of transformation. In 2018, Bloomberg Law and the

Legal Marketing Association conducted a survey in the US (admittedly, using a tiny sample compared with that in the ViewsHub survey) that indicated business development people in professional services firms were increasingly 'getting a seat at the table', as more were being asked to participate in strategic planning, business and professional development and firm leadership meetings. More than two thirds of the 190 marketers and 135 attorneys who responded to the survey said that their firms' marketing professionals were participating in these activities.[3]

As we talked more about the problem, we concluded that many of the problems to do with law firm marketing and the relationship between lawyers and marketers come from a fundamental difference in the way marketers and lawyers think. In addition, most firms are defined by a rigid distinction between fee earners and fee burners. Even more importantly, when lawyers and marketers were able to bridge that gap, they were having some terrific successes.

So, this book is designed to help marketers and business development professionals gain a more sophisticated understanding of both lawyers and law firms.

More specifically, it is designed for two types of marketers and business development professionals:

1. marketers and business development professionals who are working in law firms and struggling to get projects off the ground
2. marketers at every level of experience who are

new to law firms and finding the culture challenging or even alienating.

By taking you on a journey through the structure and culture of law firms, as well as the different ways lawyers and marketers think, this book will help you understand what makes both law firms and lawyers tick. We believe that understanding these issues will enable you to build more productive relationships with the lawyers in your firm. In short, it will help you devise strategies to undertake some internal marketing, and market yourself to the lawyers in your firm.

Nevertheless, it is important to understand this book won't provide you with a neat list of solutions that you can apply to your firm and then walk happily off into the sunset. The reality is that law firms are complex places and, if they are facing internal problems, more often than not require sophisticated solutions. This is because, even if law firms generally have many characteristics in common, every law firm is unique. The personalities that inhabit a law firm will shape both its specific culture and collective mentality. The reality is that there is never going to be a one-size-fits-all solution for every law firm.

As a result, we've designed this book so that, rather than provide superficial cookie-cutter solutions, it gives you the analytical framework to:

- gain a better understanding of both law firms and lawyers
- think about your firm, your relationship with the

lawyers you work with and how you can build
better working relationships with them

- work with the lawyers in your firm to create
marketing and business development campaigns
that deliver concrete results.

If you are in a senior leadership role or part of a management team in a firm, this book may also help you develop strategies to deal with the broader issues in your firm, whether they involve structural, cultural or personality issues (or all of the above).

We decided to join forces to write this book because we felt we had the perfect combination of experience and skills to explain the gap between lawyers and marketers and, ideally, help bridge it.

Genevieve Burnett is both a lawyer and a strategic communications specialist, so she understands the different ways lawyers and marketers think. She worked as a fee earner for seven years in one of Australia's largest independent law firms. She now helps law firms build successful digital and content marketing strategies, as well as providing them with bespoke copywriting services. She has a particular passion for improving the way lawyers communicate with their clients, especially via the written word.

Sally King is one of the most experienced marketing and communication professionals in Australia. She has a background in education, and has experience working both in government and, more recently, in law firm marketing. Over the past few years, she has built a sophisticated digital marketing strategy from the ground up. During that time, she has become adept at working with lawyers and helping them to market their services.

This book is intended to help you to build bridges between the lawyers and marketers in your firm. Even more importantly, we hope it helps you achieve your marketing goals.

With best wishes

Genevieve Burnett
PhD (UNSW) LLB (UNSW) BA(Hons) (UNSW)

Sally King
BEd (UNE) Grad Cert Marketing (UTS)

2: LAW FIRM STRUCTURE

So, you're a marketer and you've just landed a role in a law firm

If you're a marketer or business development professional who has just accepted a job in a law firm, you may feel like you have arrived in an unfamiliar world. If so, don't be alarmed, because you're not alone. We're pretty sure that just about every non-lawyer who has ever entered a law firm has felt the same way.

Interestingly, this feeling of inhabiting an alien world will probably apply whether you've accepted this new role in London, New York, Toronto or Sydney.

This is because, unless you've arrived in a funky NewLaw firm that aims to change the way law is practised and has embraced a flat business structure where everyone is equal, you will find yourself living in a world defined by hierarchy and a rigid binary distinction between fee earners and non-fee earners (sometimes referred to in firms as 'fee burners').

If your role as a marketer or business development

professional involves implementing a digital marketing strategy, you may find yourself wondering how you're going to do your job in this rather conservative environment.

To navigate the law firm you are working in, it will help if you understand how it is structured.

Most law firms are partnerships

Whether you are talking about the UK, the US or Australia, you will find that most law firms still use the business model they used 100 years ago – that is, a partnership. In the UK, most firms are limited liability partnerships but they still have the characteristics of a conventional partnership, especially in terms of how power is allocated and the way in which decisions are made.

A law firm partnership is unlike any other corporate structure. We believe the best way to grasp it is to think back to the medieval period, because most law firm partnerships have characteristics that could be described as feudal. By this, we mean that legal partnerships are structured like a pyramid and the people who work within this structure have a very clearly defined status, based on their role within the organisation.

The managing partner

In a legal partnership, the managing partner is the king or queen and sits at the top of the law firm pyramid.

As a marketer working in a law firm, you need to realise that this is a tough gig for a number of reasons. First, many lawyers who end up in managing partner roles have no training in management, leadership or finance. Instead, the reputation that has catapulted them into this role is based on their skills as a practising lawyer. Second, a managing partner never knows when their fellow partners may decide to replace them. A managing partner doesn't get to keep partners at a distance in the same way that a CEO or a chair of a board of a large, publicly listed company can keep shareholders at a distance. Instead, partners sit in the business and watch every move the managing partner makes.

At the same time, power is not necessarily evenly distributed among the partners in a law firm. For example, you may encounter a firm where power is centralised around senior management and the managing partner. You may even come across a situation where the managing partner is widely despised by the partnership but, to your surprise, you also discover that if the managing partner is on board with an idea, it will be implemented.

On the whole, however, managing partners are under constant pressure to keep their fellow partners happy. This usually means ensuring a never-ending supply of gold coins flows into their pockets. It isn't an unreasonable demand. After all, most partners have families and mortgages. At the same time, law firms have significant overheads (that is, an expensive castle to maintain). This tension between the desires of partners and the need to invest in the firm can cause problems for managing partners. For example, a managing partner may want to invest some of the firm's profits back into the business, so it can expand or so as to make significant changes. This may ruffle the feathers of their fellow equity partners, especially if it is likely to reduce their share of the firm's profits.

From the point of view of a marketer, this may mean that your managing partner keeps a close and careful watch on the marketing department's budget.

Managing partners face other challenges. The demand for legal services tends to fluctuate depending on whether the economy is expanding or shrinking. When the economy is growing, corporate does well. When times are tough, corporate slows and the litigators are busy. In a sense, law firms are always at the mercy of the market. In recent years, clients have become less willing simply to pay lawyers whatever they demand for their services. Clients now feel that they have the right to negotiate, and are less willing to accept the billable hour as the unit through which they are charged for work.

All in all, most managing partners sitting in more conventional firms find themselves constantly juggling the needs of the business with the pressure to maintain their fellow partners' bank balances. It can be tricky to manage these competing interests.

The partners

If we return to the feudal analogy, the partners in a law firm are the equivalent of aristocrats and sit at the next layer down in the pyramid.

While partners in law firms are business partners, they don't necessarily like or trust each other.

The harsh reality is that law firms around the world are full of partners who have never spoken to each other and never will. Quite often, the gap between the highest- and lowest-earning members of a partnership is vast. Many partners start life as salaried partners, and will only be made equity partners if they meet or exceed budget. In addition, many partners find themselves in direct competition for business with the other partners in their own firm. When client business continues to shrink, the growing threat of de-equitisation hangs over every partner (with the exception of those within the inner circle of management). A large number of firms periodically undergo 'clean-outs' that resemble totalitarian purges. In short, life in a law firm isn't just the fat cats sitting around licking the cream.

As a marketer, the first thing you may notice about your law firm is that most partners have an autocratic management style that is all about issuing commands and having control.

Jil Toovey is Director of IKD and has spent nearly 20 years helping lawyers develop their leadership skills. We spoke to Jil because we knew she could help us unravel some of the structural and cultural problems that were challenging marketers in law firms, and preventing the firms from developing firm-wide marketing strategies and adapting to the digital era.

Jil explained to us that lawyers are generally under significant pressure to get work to clients promptly. The drive to get results and deliver to clients can mean that, as professionals, they have strong controlling tendencies. The problem with the controlling style of management is that 'if you are controlling someone, you can't actually connect with them'. In short, the task takes precedence over the relationship.

Jil went on to describe the case of one partner she worked with, the results of whose 360 review showed that he was perceived as being very controlling. She asked him to think back to a situation where he was really under the pump and getting work out the door. She then asked him to describe how he interacted with his team. The partner explained that he was simply pushing the work out. Jil asked him about the lawyers coming into his office, what their names were and how they were coping. The partner reflected on the question for some time and then said that the lawyers were 'faceless, like shadows'. He then said that he had no idea what the lawyers felt about the work because, at that moment, he was in machine mode.

We also spoke to Avril Henry, an internationally acclaimed expert in transforming leadership. With a background in information technology (IT), human resources (HR) and change management in South Africa,

Australia, the UK and the US, Avril has worked in-house in both the legal and banking sectors. More recently, she's been widely acclaimed for her work in achieving a change in leadership style and culture in the Australian Army. We knew she would be able to throw still more light on the question of leadership in law firms.

Avril confirmed that law firms operate on a command-and-control style of leadership. In her time with law firms, she conducted dozens and dozens of coaching sessions with both partners and lawyers. She told us that:

> *Those sessions showed that the vast majority of partners had the following traits. First, they didn't listen because they were too busy telling. Second, they had no interest in how other people saw them. Third, they were verbally aggressive.*

She went on to explain that, 'The command-and-control style of leadership is based on fear and intimidation. It doesn't get the best out of people, because they usually respond by shutting down.'

The lawyers: the fee earners

The lawyers, or fee earners, in a law firm are like the tradespeople or merchants in a feudal society. Most are hoping that, one day, they will be rewarded for their hard work with an aristocratic title (or welcomed into the partnership). The lawyers sit in the middle of the law firm pyramid. They have more privileges than those below them because they earn fees, which go into the pockets of the equity partners in return for a salary.

However, anyone who spends a number of years working in a law firm will notice that only a small percentage of lawyers ever make partner. This creates a certain amount of dysfunction within the firm because lawyers often have to work in teams, especially if the firm has been retained to assist with a large matter or transaction. However, at the same time as the lawyers work together for the sake of a client, they are competitors. This means that lawyers tend to avoid building close or meaningful relationships with their colleagues. After all, it doesn't make sense to share your vulnerabilities with someone who could eventually use them against you.

The non-professionals: the fee burners

Everyone else in a law firm is called a 'non-professional', even if they are university educated. This includes marketers and business development professionals.

In a law firm, a professional is defined as someone who bills clients for their work. Fee burners include support staff as well as staff working in finance, operations, IT and HR, and the business development and marketing team.

In most law firms, you will find that the marketing and business development team, like HR, finance, operations and IT, is situated separately from the rest of the firm. This can create the 'us' and 'them' mentality in law firms that causes a cultural gap, as well as miscommunication. It also reinforces the fee earner/fee burner paradigm.

The exception to the rule: C-Suite officers

For every rule, there is an exception. In larger firms, the exception to the fee burner rule may include a small, elite group of non-lawyers that may take on roles in the C-Suite (such as the chief operating officer, the chief financial officer and the chief marketing officer).

Over the years, as the practice of law has become more commercialised, lawyers have discovered that they don't necessarily have all the answers when it comes to running a business, so have increasingly reached out for expert assistance to the world of finance and management consulting. In terms of the feudal structure, these people are like ambassadors from abroad and their position in the firm depends on how much respect they can earn from the partners. The partnership will seek their counsel when it suits them. However, a non-legal C-Suite executive may find that their advice is ignored and, if the weather changes suddenly, that their services are no longer needed.

Nevertheless, C-Suite executives will have more clout than the average non-lawyer. In fact, we've seen some chief marketing officers and chief operating officers launch some pretty impressive digital marketing campaigns, simply because they had the clout and saw an opportunity.

Can adopting an alternative business structure (ABS) transform a law firm's culture?

At present, there are only two jurisdictions outside the US that allow law firms to use ABSs – England and Wales, and Australia. In the US, only the District of Columbia (DC) allows a limited form of ABS. Relatively few ABS law firms have organised in the DC area because DC attorneys are often licensed in one or more jurisdictions and no other US jurisdiction allows ABSs. This makes it an unattractive option for any firm that may plan to expand outside the DC.[4]

In 2007, the UK's *Legal Services Act* established ABSs and allowed non-lawyers to hold professional management or ownership roles in law firms for the first time. As we've mentioned above, the challenge in the past had been that, with the traditional or feudal model, law firms expected people who were great legal technicians to do many other tasks that were needed to run a business, such as those to do with sales, business development and billing activities. The idea behind ABSs was that they would be more flexible and allow non-lawyers to become co-owners in the business. In turn, this would mean that, especially if they were start-ups, ABS firms would be more likely to be innovative and adopt new technologies that would put them at an advantage compared with traditional firms.[5]

In 2001, New South Wales became the first state in Australia to allow ABSs, which are called incorporated legal practices (ILPs). Victoria, Queensland and Western Australia soon followed. It wasn't long before thousands of ILPs were operating across the country. Today, around 30% of Australian law firms are ILPs.

With solicitor directors instead of partners, ILPs sound much more modern and corporate, and there is no doubt that some firms have adopted a more progressive approach to the way they run their businesses as a result of becoming ILPs.

We believe that when you find a law firm to be innovative and progressive, it will almost always have adopted an ABS. That said, just because a law firm has adopted an ABS doesn't mean it will automatically become innovative and progressive.

This is due to the reality that the adoption of a new business structure doesn't necessarily change the culture of a law firm or the mentality of the lawyers working in that firm, especially if they have been raised in the traditional firm environment. Rather, in the vast majority of cases, the people in these firms tend to cling to the culture and mentality of a conventional partnership because that is the culture and mentality with which they are familiar and comfortable.

This means that firms that adopt ABSs in order to become more innovative cannot rely on the change in structure alone. Rather, they also need to change the culture that defines not only their values but their mode of operation.

Nevertheless, the key point about a law firm being

founded on, or moving to, an ABS is that this structure, unlike the traditional partnership model, provides a framework where there is more of a chance that a culture of innovation and change can flourish.

How can you develop powerful marketing campaigns if you're working for a partnership that is based on a rigid hierarchy?

If you're a marketer or business development professional, the question at this point is: how do you navigate this rigid hierarchy and get concrete results from your marketing strategies?

First, you need to ensure you don't take your technical status as a 'fee burner' personally. It is something that has emerged out of the traditional business structure that law firms use. We suggest you focus on demonstrating to the fee earners how you can contribute value, and do your best to ensure that the communication channels between you and the lawyers in your firm are as open as possible.

Second, you should form strong alliances with those partners and lawyers in the firm who understand and appreciate the importance of marketing and business development. This means that you can use the work you do with these fee earners as an example to those fee earners who are more sceptical about the value of marketing. In addition, they can act as your supporters and advocates when key decisions are about to be made at the management level.

Third, you need to appreciate that lawyers have a great deal of respect for evidence.

In order to help partners and lawyers see the way their business is structured and how it limits their ability to launch innovative marketing strategies, you can show them examples of successful strategies that other firms have launched and use these to build support for any strategy you wish to implement.

3: LAW FIRM CULTURE

The decision-making process in law firms can be slow

As a marketer, you may find that the decision-making process in law firms is slower than you are used to in other corporate structures.

Lawyers tend to like process and consultation. The trouble is that slow and cumbersome processes with too many checks and balances kill any kind of innovation.

When we talked to Jil Toovey, she agreed that the structure of most law firms is still very hierarchical, and went on to point out their decision-making process was often slow and inefficient compared with that of other corporate entities. This is because, in a partnership, you are dealing with many business owners with strong and, at times, conflicting points of view.

Jil went on to point out the absurdity of the decision-making process in many law firms when she explained that, 'if an idea actually isn't torn to shreds in a meeting, it can take weeks to wind its way up and down the hierarchy'. She gave an example of a firm she worked with that was evaluating which particular 360 review tool they should use in a leadership development program for their lawyers. As an expert in the area, she recommended a specific product. Before deciding, management tasked someone with researching every 360 review tool on the market. After six weeks, they came back to her, agreeing with the initial proposal. Jil believes that these tendencies come from the risk-averse nature of the legal profession, and its need for extensive research, evidence and precedent before feeling able to make a confident decision.

We also talked to Avril Henry about the process of decision-making in law firms. She was quick to point out that, 'One of the biggest problems with a partnership is that you can have up to 170 owners of the business (depending on the size of the organisation) with the right to comment and vote on any major change. This makes any change very difficult to achieve.'

Law firms stifle dissent and reward conformity

Another interesting characteristic of traditional law firms is that they tend to reward conformity and punish dissent.

Jil Toovey said that her experiences working both in-house and consulting to law firms confirmed this. She recalled an HR professional telling her about a talented lawyer who joined the firm, and who was lively, confident and very independent in his thinking. He spoke up in meetings even though he was very junior. This did not go down well. The partners instructed the HR professional to tell him to 'tone it down'. Ultimately, his style was deemed unsuitable for the firm and he was moved on.

We also talked to Avril Henry about conformity in law firms. She, too, said that law firms are notorious for rewarding conformity. 'The tragedy of this for law firms', she explained, 'is that problem-solving never comes from conformity. Instead, it comes from valuing difference and diversity of thought.'

Law firms often nurture a bullying culture

The bullying culture that exists within law firms is well known and has been widely discussed. After all, most junior lawyers have experienced a senior lawyer or partner yelling at them for messing up. If they haven't experienced it personally, they've seen or heard it.

In 2012, the Law Council of Australia undertook the *National Attrition and Re-engagement Study*, which focused on the drivers of the attrition of women from the legal profession nationally. One in two women and more than one in three men reported having been bullied or intimidated in their current workplace.[6]

According to the American Bar Association, which looked at the Australian research, the situation is similar in the US.[7] The consensus is that this may have something to do with the profession being both fast-paced and adversarial in nature.

Jil Toovey says she believes that bullying is at times an unconscious component of the legal psyche. She was involved in research relating to magistrates in Australia and what they wanted to see from lawyers appearing before them. This revealed specific beliefs and assumptions that drove the magistrates' interactions with lawyers in their courts. The interviews showed that, predominantly, they lacerate young lawyers from the bench because they perceive the law to be a tough profession and they feel it is their duty to toughen up the lawyers to ensure they survive. She thinks that this attitude is definitely changing, with the growing consciousness of the importance of wellbeing and mental health within the profession, but believes that, on the whole, change is slower in the law than in other professions.

Former Australian High Court justice Michael Kirby has said that he believes judges' rudeness trickles down to junior lawyers in a cycle of bullying and stress that is rife within the legal profession.[8]

We would argue that there is a disconnect in the profession in Australia. On one hand, there is much discussion of the need to eliminate a bullying culture. On the other, it is very much business as usual, especially when the individual engaging in bullying behaviours is a significant fee earner.

We asked Avril Henry how she had managed to work so effectively with the Australian Army and, more specifically, Lieutenant-General David Morrison, the former chief of army, to eradicate a bullying culture and establish one which required everyone to live up to a core set of values. She explained that:

> *While there was commitment from the highest levels to change the values of the army and eradicate inappropriate behaviour, the underlying reality is that the army is subject to public scrutiny and also accountable for what goes on within it. In a sense, the Australian Army was forced to change. Law firms, in contrast, aren't subject to the same kind of public scrutiny. Nor are they as accountable for what goes on within them.*

Law firms and mental health

There is little doubt that the hierarchical structure of law firms not only enables a culture where bullying can flourish but also plays a role in creating an environment where a large number of lawyers end up suffering from mental illness.

In the US, the statistics show that the legal profession is prone to higher incidences of depression than the general population. As many as one in four lawyers suffers from psychological distress, including anxiety, social alienation, isolation and depression.[9] According to a study of more than 100 occupations, undertaken by researchers at Johns Hopkins University, lawyers have the highest incidence of depression in the nation. In 1996, lawyers overtook dentists as the profession with the highest rate of suicide. The American Bar Association estimates that

15–20% of lawyers suffer from alcoholism and engage in substance abuse. In addition, seven out of ten lawyers responding to a *Californian Lawyer* magazine poll said they would change professions if the opportunity arose.[10]

In 2016, a study that surveyed 12,825 American lawyers and was published in the *Journal of Addiction Medicine* showed that 28% of respondents suffered from depression, 19% suffered from anxiety and 20% 'screened positive for hazardous, harmful and potentially alcohol-dependent drinking'.[11]

High rates of mental illness among lawyers aren't confined to the US.

In the UK, a 2012 survey of the legal profession conducted by LawCare revealed that more than 50% of the profession felt stressed and 19% were suffering from clinical depression. That is, one fifth of the profession was suffering from (mostly) avoidable and preventable mental ill-health issues. In 2013, the UK Law Society interviewed 2,226 solicitors about stress at work and, shockingly, more than 95% said their stress was extreme or severe. Even more alarmingly, 36% of stressed-out calls to LawCare in 2014 were from solicitors who had less than five years of post-qualification experience, indicating that even lawyers at the beginning of their careers are feeling extreme pressure and stress.[12]

Some of the most comprehensive research into the mental health of the legal profession has been undertaken in Australia, and legal professionals here report higher levels of depressive symptoms when compared with the general population. In a pattern that is similar to the one in the US, those working in law firms indicated higher rates of depressive symptoms when compared with the other professional groups examined, such as accountants, IT professionals, architects, actuaries, insurance underwriters and brokers.[13]

In 2008, a study that the Brain and Mind Centre at the University of Sydney conducted showed that depression affected 33% of solicitors and 20% of barristers.[14] In addition, the study indicated that around 11% of lawyers contemplated suicide each month and 15% met the criteria for alcoholism.[15]

In 2011, another study showed that 47% of solicitors and 42% of barristers admitted to suffering depression. In short, the research indicated that lawyers in Australia had much higher levels of distress than the general community.[16] In an even more alarming trend, there is research that indicates 86% of legal professionals would prefer to suffer in silence than disclose a mental health condition, from fear of being fired or passed over for promotion.[17]

In Canada, the situation in relation to lawyers' mental health is similar. In 2017 Professor Ronit Dinovitzer of the University of Toronto undertook research based on results of a survey conducted by the Canadian Bar Association that showed the more lawyers got paid, the more likely they were to experience depression and dissatisfaction with their career choice and to face a work-life balance conflict. In addition, this research showed that Canadian lawyers from elite law schools who were working at the most prestigious law firms and making the most income reported higher levels of depression, lower levels of career-choice satisfaction, and an intention to leave their much-sought-after positions in the short term.[18]

The generational division in law firms

You can see that the structure and culture of law firms mean that the dynamics of the average law firm are complex. However, the situation is currently even more challenging because, for the first time, law firms have to manage four generations:

1. silents or traditionalists
2. baby boomers
3. Generation X (Gen X)
4. Millennials or Generation Y (Gen Y).[19]

Law firms, like other businesses, are also about to welcome a new generation, Gen Z, or iGen, who were born around 1996, and are about to graduate from university and enter the profession.

For marketers and business development professionals, it is vital to understand the attitudes and expectations of the various generations.

Silents or traditionalists
These days silents or traditionalists (born between 1925 and 1946) are fairly rare in law firms but they are still around.

They tend to be loyal workers. They are dedicated, but also risk averse because their values were shaped by the Depression, World War II and the post-war boom years. As senior partners in law firms, they believe in team work, in the sense that everyone should work as hard as they did to become a partner. These days, silents or traditionalists probably don't interact with the rest of their firms very much. They have their clients, do their work and try to ensure that, when they retire, they have enough money to do so comfortably.

As a marketer or business development professional, you will probably find that a silent or traditionalist is sceptical about marketing, and resistant to embracing or investing in new technology. You may even find that a silent or traditionalist clings to the idea of law being a respectable profession and is reluctant to see it as a business.

Baby boomers

Baby boomers (born between 1946 and 1964) tend to value work over personal life. Their values were shaped by growing up in a tumultuous time in history, which included the Vietnam War. They are more open to change than a silent or a traditionalist may be, but they are also part of the Me Generation. This means that they have always openly pursued personal gratification. Baby boomers have a strong work ethic and are self-assured, competitive, goal-oriented and disciplined. Following the dot.com crash and the Global Financial Crisis, their retirement savings may have been reduced and they may be working for longer than they planned. They may even be considering working part-time in retirement or not retiring at all. This may be because they like working or they need to replace their lost retirement savings.

Baby boomers are loyal to the firm they work for, and it is quite possible they have worked there for their entire professional life. Like the generation above them, they worked very hard to become partners. As junior lawyers, the partners they worked for probably expected them to do extremely long hours. They now expect the same kind of dedication from their junior lawyers.

As a leader, the baby boomer's management style is command and control. They are often surprised when junior staff members leave, because they can't imagine giving up the chance to become a partner.

It is quite likely that a given baby boomer partner has had a mid-life crisis between the ages of 45 and 50, when they started to wonder what they had been doing for the last 25 years.

These days, they leave work early and expect their junior lawyers to work late.

As a marketer or business development professional, you may find that baby boomer partners are a little more receptive to the concept of marketing the firm. After all, most baby boomers joined law firms during the 1970s and 1980s, as firms became more commercialised, and introduced marketing and business development teams. Nevertheless, you may find that baby boomer partners are still not quite convinced of the value of marketing for law firms, because that function has mostly always been siloed.

Gen X

Gen X (born between 1965 and 1980) have a tendency to question authority figures, such as the baby boomer partner they work for, and to place high value on the concept of work-life balance. Their baby boomer boss may think they are less dedicated, but Gen X are willing to take on challenges and able to adapt to job instability.

It is quite likely a member of Gen X had their first mid-life crisis in their early 30s and decided to re-invent themselves. If they are now in their 40s, they may be considering doing this again.

Gen X are loyal to people rather than firms. This means that if a Gen X lawyer works for a great partner and that person moves elsewhere, they will be keen to follow them.

We are now at the point where Gen X are taking over the leadership of law firms. All the evidence indicates that this will lead to a change in style of leadership. Unlike the silents or traditionalists and baby boomers, Gen X are willing to challenge the ideas of their predecessors. For example, they are more interested in employing collaborative styles of leadership, rather than the old command-and-control method, because they understand that this gets better results and means that law firms have a better chance of retaining staff.

Most importantly for marketers and business development professionals, members of Gen X are likely to take marketing and business development more seriously than their predecessors did.

Millennials (Gen Y)

Millennials (born between 1980 and 1995) tend to have a very global outlook because they came of age during the rapid growth of the internet and the increase in global terrorism. They are very resilient in navigating change, while having an appreciation of diversity and inclusion. They work well in a team because their parents, so as to focus on work, programmed much of their lives with activities such as sports and music. They are willing to work hard to achieve the lifestyle they want. At the same time, they expect to be rewarded for being tech savvy.

Millennials are unlikely to put up with an abusive boss or a work culture that they don't enjoy. They are looking to work for someone who has a collaborative or inclusive style of leadership. They want to be heard and to participate in the decision-making process. Their favourite question is 'Why?' because they want to understand why things are done a certain way. However, a baby boomer partner may interpret this as a direct challenge to their authority.

The above traits are demonstrated by the fact that, instead of putting up with life as a miserable lawyer working for a bullying partner, a Millennial will leave and even set up their own business. This means that the other generations see them as demanding and picky.

Consequently, Millennials are always reinventing themselves because they are comfortable with change even if they want consistency in their personal life.

From the perspective of a marketing or business development professional, Millennial lawyers would seem to be excellent potential allies in law firms. After all, Millennials understand social media and the concept of self-promotion. At the same time, they may be over-confident because they believe they are the techno generation, which means that working with them produces its own set of challenges.

The generational divide makes marketing a law firm even more of a challenge

There is no doubt that the fact we currently have four generations working within a feudal structure makes life even more challenging for anyone in a law firm, especially when it comes to change, innovation and using new technologies.

Dealing with four generations, along with the normal politics that shape law firm life, makes it difficult to build consensus. It can be challenging to create a business development or marketing strategy that satisfies the expectations and objectives of four generations of lawyers.

When we talked to Avril Henry, who has become an expert in the role the different generations play in the workplace and in how to manage the resulting tensions, she pointed out that 'While baby boomers and the older members of Gen X often adopt a command-and-control style of leadership, this doesn't sit well with Millennials, who expect leadership by example.' She added, 'Gen Y expect their leaders to listen and be collaborative. They want to work for people they like and respect, and who respect them as people in return.'

We believe that law firms are having difficulty embracing marketing and adjusting to the digital era not only because of their structure (which makes it difficult for them to adapt to change) but because they become impotent when trying to satisfy the needs and expectations of multiple generations.

How can you overcome the challenges associated with working in such a conservative and fragmented workplace culture?

There is no doubt that the cultural issues in law firms make life for marketers and business development professionals challenging. Nevertheless, there are a number of strategies you can employ not only to achieve better results but to ensure that you build strong relationships with the lawyers you work with.

First, as a marketer who is used to trying and testing strategies quickly, you need to be patient and even have a steely resolve if you are working in a law firm. In short, working in law firm marketing is a marathon rather than a sprint. You also need to accept that developing and introducing marketing strategies may take longer than you expect. In the end, you need to realise that lawyers are smart and you will always have a good chance of winning them with a great idea or strategy.

Second, you need to be tough, especially if you are operating in a law firm where bullying is a part of the culture. The good news is that there is much more awareness of the detrimental effects of bullying, and evidence to suggest that it is on the decline in most law firms, especially in those where Gen X is taking over the leadership roles.

Third, any marketer or business development professional should take into account that they are probably working in an environment where the lawyers are under a great deal of pressure. In addition, you may be working with legal professionals who are suffering from clinical depression. As a result, you will need to be sensitive to the pressures they face, and should try to make their lives easier rather than harder. This means that you may need to think about the appropriate time to approach someone regarding a particular issue or problem, or find ways to reduce the amount of work involved in implementing a particular marketing strategy. In short, you don't want to add to the stress of people who are already under a great deal of stress.

Finally, you need to be aware of the different attitudes, values and expectations of the different generations of lawyers in your law firm. You need to consider these, especially when you are putting together a business development plan for an individual lawyer.

4: MEET THE LAWYERS

The great thing about working with lawyers is that they're both smart and hardworking.

Broadly speaking, from our experience working for and with law firms, and talking to both lawyers and marketers, it is possible to identify five types of lawyers working in firms:

1. the dinosaur
2. the laser beam
3. the salesperson
4. the rock star
5. the introverted professional.

From a marketer's perspective, some types are easier to work with than others.

The dinosaur

Most law firms still contain a few dinosaurs.

A legal dinosaur has probably been at the firm for their entire professional life, and wants to continue practising law in the way they have since they entered the profession in the 1960s or 1970s. Dinosaurs inspire a mixture of fear, respect and even a drop of affection in their colleagues, even if everyone secretly wonders when they're going to hang up their hat and walk out the door. Nevertheless, the term 'dinosaur' refers to a mentality or attitude, rather than the age of a particular practitioner. That being said, most dinosaurs will be silents or traditionalists, or baby boomers.

More often than not, the dinosaur's primary interest is to secure the largest possible golden handshake when they leave the firm in the next few years. For that reason, they don't like spending money on anything that is likely to reduce the size of it. However, they would never say that is why they are blocking every new initiative that is likely to require a substantial investment of time and money.

A dinosaur may be the kind of partner who believes that junior lawyers and any non-lawyer at the firm should be seen rather than heard, because that is how they were treated. They may believe that anyone who messes up should be eaten for breakfast.

Dinosaurs will have little interest in technology; in many cases, their personal assistant does their typing and sends emails on their behalf. They are suspicious of the word 'marketing' simply because they built their practice mostly through referrals and their personal network. Quite often, their personal network is based on the old school tie.

The laser beam

The second type of lawyer is the legal laser beam.

The laser beam is passionate about law. They find it intellectually interesting and challenging. In a way, these are the true lawyers because they have an uncanny ability to analyse legal issues with extreme precision, as well as come up with solutions to complex legal problems. Ideally, a legal laser beam will be commercially astute, which means that they will understand their clients' business drivers, as well as their commercial objectives.

It goes without saying that legal laser beams are very good at what they do. However, more often than not, they have no real interest in marketing, or may even be dismissive of it, because their main objective is to sit in their offices and use the law to realise their clients' dreams or solve their problems.

The legal salesperson

The third type of lawyer we've identified is the legal salesperson.

Legal salespersons are not as bewitched by the practice of law as are the laser beams. Quite possibly, law doesn't interest them as much as it should but they see it as a means to an end. Legal salespersons are good with people. They are social creatures, so they make great lunch companions or drinking buddies. They are active on social media platforms such as LinkedIn and are always keen to attend a junket where they can promote their wares.

Quite often, legal salespersons aren't the most skilled or incisive practitioners in the firm. However, they are perfectly satisfactory. Their greatest skill is their confidence, especially when they are dealing with clients. It should be noted that most legal laser beams think legal salespersons are nothing more than charlatans, and resent their ability to attract clients. The tension between laser beams and salespersons makes life in a law firm interesting.

The downfall of many legal salespersons is that they have a tendency always to be on the lookout for the bigger and better client.

As a marketer, you are not going to have much trouble convincing the legal salespersons that they need to market themselves. Rather, the challenge will be persuading them that their favourite marketing strategy may not be the most effective. More specifically, in the digital era, hiring that very expensive corporate box at a sporting event may be less effective than proving themselves expert in a particular area by writing articles or presenting seminars.

This is because the emergence of the digital world means clients have become more sophisticated in the way they select their legal service providers. You can no longer rely on the old school tie or your mutual love of sport. After all, in 2014, women made up 43% of practising lawyers in Australia, and we suspect that those who work as in-house counsel will be unlikely to select their external legal service advisor based on the social aspects of the relationship.[20] It is also worth noting that, currently, 61% of solicitors admitted in Australia are women, so there is little doubt that the profession is becoming increasingly feminised and the traditional ways of attracting clients are transforming.[21] The situation is similar in the UK, where women make up 48% of all lawyers in law firms.[22] In the US, the percentage is lower, with women making up 34.6% of members of the American Bar Association.[23]

The rock star

The fourth type of lawyer is the legal rock star, who is rarer than laser beams or salespersons.

The talent of the legal rock star is the way they combine the skills of the legal laser beam with those of the salesperson. In short, rock stars are the complete package because not only is their legal work superb but clients like to talk to them. They are the ultimate 'trusted advisors' and, as a result, tend to be the rainmakers in their firms.

They run their teams like a business. These partners know how much their time costs them, and how much they are paying their business development and marketing team. They know the value of good people-management practices and of retaining high-quality staff.

Most importantly, legal rock stars understand digital,

and use it to promote themselves and the service they offer clients.

Rather than being intimidated by a legal rock star, we suggest that if you work in a business development or marketing role, these lawyers are your greatest assets and potential allies. After all, in any job, especially if it involves change management, it always helps to have allies. As a result, legal rock stars are the ideal people with whom to build alliances within the firm, so they can help you get your business development and marketing projects across the line.

The introverted professional

The fifth type of lawyer is the introverted professional.

These lawyers are intelligent, industrious and efficient, but tend to fly under the radar because they are quiet and understated. In short, in law firms they are usually overshadowed by their more extroverted colleagues. This means that only a few people in the firm will be aware of the introverted professional's achievements because firms tend to notice and reward behaviour that is characteristic of extroverts.

As a result, the introverted professional is often overlooked, especially by marketing and business development teams, because they don't brag about their achievements. Instead, they focus on powering through the work, meeting budget and keeping their clients happy.

The introverted professional builds teams with

similarly minded lawyers. For that reason, the entire team may find itself overlooked within the firm.

In the digital era, the personality traits of the introverted professional can be a major challenge. After all, we now live in a world where lawyers need to promote themselves on social media platforms such as LinkedIn. However, the introverted professional, irrespective of their age, has little interest in the modern tools of self-promotion. As a result, they may find that a more extroverted professional with an impressive online presence comes along and 'steals their lunch'.

The lawyer who is about to be deleted

Jil Toovey helped us identify another type of lawyer. She calls him 'David'.

David is the lawyer who the partner has identified as hopeless based on the one task they have completed unsatisfactorily. Their story is as follows. When David first arrived at the firm, the partner gave him a task and he did not do it very well. As a result, the partner no longer gives work to David. When someone suggests David for a particular task, the partner now says, 'Not David', and that attitude spreads like a virus around the team. Soon, David isn't getting any work from anyone and his billable hours are plummeting.

Jil explained that when she encountered these kinds of cases, she would go to the partner and ask them, 'So, what is the problem with David?' The partner would explain what had occurred and she would ask, 'Did you talk to David? Did you give him any feedback on his work? Did you explain what was wrong with it?' The response from the partner would be, 'No, it's easier to use someone who is technically competent.'

Meanwhile, David's career is going down the gurgler faster than he can say, 'I love being a lawyer.'

In our experience, lawyers who leave law firms in these kinds of circumstances are never talked about again. One day, they've gone and their offices are empty. In short, they are deleted.

'Davids' are probably of little interest to marketers or business development professionals, who have little to do with them. After all, 'Davids' are usually at the early stages of their career, and are focusing on developing their legal skills rather than marketing them. Nevertheless, in terms of understanding a working environment that can be brutal, marketers and business development professionals need to be aware that 'Davids' are reasonably common in law firms. They provide a good example of the pressures lawyers face and the fact that law firms can be brutal.

How should you approach working with different types of lawyers?

As a marketer or business development professional, you need to adapt how you work with lawyers, according to their professional strengths and weaknesses.

The first step in this process is identifying the kind of lawyer you are working with. Obviously, lawyers are people, and people are complex. As a result, you are probably going to find that not all lawyers fit perfectly into the categories we've identified above. Nevertheless, we believe they are a useful framework for identifying not only the strengths and weaknesses of lawyers, but how to devise a marketing strategy that is tailored specifically to the individual you are working with.

When it comes to working with legal dinosaurs, we expect that you will find they won't have a great deal of interest in marketing or business development for two reasons. First, they were not raised in an environment where marketing was an important business activity. Second, their careers are winding down, so they have little need or desire to market their services. The most important thing to realise is that these lawyers have usually achieved a great deal in their careers and that you need to be respectful of those achievements. You may even discover that the lawyer who everyone regards as a dinosaur has played a key role in building the firm. As a result, it may be worth your while to make the effort to talk to these lawyers because they have a lot of experience in practising law, as well as in dealing with clients. In short, we suggest that, if the opportunity arises, you mine them for their insights into the profession.

The laser beam lawyer is probably someone a marketing or business development professional is going to encounter quite frequently. When working with laser beams, we suggest your role should be to educate these lawyers so that they not only see the value of marketing and business development but understand the importance of using marketing techniques to promote the services they offer. We suggest you focus on nurturing their talent, and use the marketing strategies that are most suited to their skills. For example, you may find that a laser beam lawyer is more suited to writing articles and promoting their skills via content marketing than to attending net-working events. In the end, it is about finding the right strategy to help the legal laser beam feel more comfort-able with marketing and business development.

When working with the legal salesperson, you are probably not going to have much trouble persuading them of the importance and value of marketing and business development. The trick here is to ensure that the quality of their efforts to market themselves is up to scratch. For example, if a legal salesperson writes an article, you will need to ensure that it is of a standard that will reflect well on them as a professional, as well as the firm, because they may have a tendency to rush work when they are busy.

For a marketer or business development profes-sional, the ideal lawyer to work with is the legal rock star. After all, legal rock stars are talented practitioners who also understand the need to promote themselves in the market for legal services. The challenge for marketers and business professionals, who are often incredibly busy, is to find the time to develop the best possible strategy to help legal rock stars sell their services to prospective clients. As we've mentioned above, legal rock stars are valuable potential allies for marketers and business development professionals because they can be used as examples of the effectiveness of particular marketing strategies.

Although legal rock stars may be the easiest lawyers to work with, we also encourage you to make the effort to find and nurture the introverted professionals in your firm. As with the laser beam, you will need to identify the marketing tools most suited to publicising their skills and talents. Most importantly, you should take the time to let them know that you are aware of their achievements and explain the importance of lifting their public profile, especially in cyberspace.

With introverted professionals, you may also need to change the way you work. For example, if you organise a brainstorming session that includes an introverted professional, you may find that they won't speak in a large group. For that reason, you want to give them more time to think about what is being discussed, or break a larger team into smaller groups to encourage the introvert to share their ideas. This will mean that you still capture the idea, but a more extroverted member of the smaller group can present the idea to the larger team.

5: HOW LAWYERS THINK

Lawyers don't necessarily make good leaders

Although most lawyers think they are natural leaders, this isn't necessarily true. As we have already pointed out, the feudal culture of law firms encourages a rather authoritarian leadership style where partners get used to giving commands and expect everyone else to follow those commands without question. This trait can become even more entrenched in managing partners. In addition, most partners keep their cards close to their chests, which means that there tends to be a lack of clear communication.

As we've already explained, most lawyers don't have a good understanding of leadership and how it feeds into management. Many lawyers thrust into leadership roles lack emotional intelligence, particularly empathy and self-awareness, which are vital for good leadership.

This means that, as a marketer or business development professional, you may need to develop a thick skin, and realise that any inappropriate behaviour may be due to a partner missing a sensitivity chip rather than them deliberately setting out to hurt your feelings.

Lawyers like to manage by objectives

When we talked to Jil Toovey, she explained that most lawyers like to manage by objectives. However, when you are dealing with an area where there aren't any right or wrong answers, lawyers struggle because they're paid 'to know and to be right'. When a lawyer doesn't 'know' the answer and it can't be located in a statute, precedent or textbook, they become uncomfortable because their professional identity is strongly connected to being an expert.

When working with lawyers in a marketing or business development context on a problem that does not have a finite answer, you may need to take the time to explain to them that coming up with the right answer may involve an element of trial and error.

Many lawyers are perfectionists

Many lawyers are perfectionists. Perfectionism is a particularly difficult trait to deal with because, on one hand, the perfectionist appears to be very confident, even arrogant. At the same time, their internal critic is telling them, 'You are hopeless. Nothing you do is good enough. Nothing you achieve will ever be enough.'

Perfectionists are at greater risk of burnout, as they tend to set excessively high performance standards they inevitably fail to meet, which in turn diminishes their sense of personal accomplishment.[24] Professor Gordon Parker, Scientia Professor of Psychiatry at the University of New South Wales in Sydney and former Executive Director of the Black Dog Institute, says that perfectionists frequently use black-and-white thinking, which involves the belief 'I've got to solve the problem immediately or there's no way out.' In short, they tend not to see a third or fourth option.[25]

As a marketer or business development professional, you need to become skilled at working with perfectionists. More specifically, you need to emphasise to them that perfection is not required and that it is important to explore a broad range of options when looking for a solution.

Lawyers don't like non-billable work

Lawyers working in private practice are under considerable pressure to meet their budgets. Billing in most firms is based on six-minute units, meaning that there are ten units in an hour. Depending on the firm, most lawyers are expected to bill clients between six and seven hours per day. This is on top of any non-billable work they have to complete.

Lawyers who exceed budget are rewarded with salary rises and are then on their way to being made partners. In contrast, those who fail to meet budget can find themselves missing out on pay rises. They may even find themselves warned that they should pull up their socks (even if they've spent time undertaking valuable tasks that aren't billable).

The pressure to bill is very deeply ingrained in lawyers. From the minute they walk in the door as young lawyers, it is the most important thing in their professional lives. As a lawyer, you are either behind, on or ahead of, budget.

To make matters even more interesting, most electronic time management systems that law firms use are designed to allow lawyers to spy on each other. From the point of view of management, this is ideal because lawyers who are competing with each other will constantly try to bill more than their colleagues. However, it is hardly conducive to team building and, as we've already mentioned, lawyers often have to work in teams.

The emphasis on billable work in law firms is problematic for a range of reasons. It encourages inefficiency because, technically, the longer it takes a lawyer to complete a task, the greater the financial reward they will receive. The stories about lawyers fudging their timesheets in an attempt to meet or exceed budget are legendary.

From the point of view of the fee earner/fee burner paradigm, the emphasis on billing in law firms means that non-billable work becomes something that most lawyers resent because it distracts them from billing clients. In short, lawyers look down on such work because it can't be measured easily in dollars and cents. As a result, lawyers either try to employ non-lawyers to do this work or outsource it to non-lawyers.

Ultimately, and most importantly, this leads lawyers to look at the people in law firms who perform work that isn't billable as second-class citizens. Another consequence of this attitude is that key aspects of the business are constantly neglected simply because they are not seen as a priority.

The importance of billable work in law firms is something every marketer and business development professional needs to understand and appreciate. After all, the reality is that the fees extracted from clients pay everyone's salaries. For this reason, it is important to be respectful of a lawyer's need to bill fees, and to make a conscious effort to work around the time pressures that lawyers face due to the constant pressure of billable work.

Lawyers are risk averse

Lawyers think differently from other professionals. Law teaches you to analyse problems in a very specific way and it can narrow your view of the world. As a lawyer, you can't help dissecting most issues from a legal perspective.

There also seems to be something about studying law that inhibits the ability to think outside the box and creates an aversion to risk, as well as a reluctance to stand out from the crowd.

Once a young lawyer enters the legal profession, the aversion to risk increases rather than diminishes. After all, lawyers spend most of their lives identifying risk or finding ways to reduce it.

It is also worth noting that law is a conservative profession, steeped in history. In the UK and Australia (as well as in many other Commonwealth countries), barristers and judges still wear robes. This goes back to the fourteenth century, when lawyers retained the tunic that scholars wore as a sign of learning. Although the tunic was initially brightly coloured, on the death of Charles II, in 1685, the bar went into a period of mourning and barristers began to wear mourning gowns. This is the origin of the black gown that barristers wear today.[26] Yes, the tradition is, quite literally, feudal.

In the Anglo-American world, the legal systems are based on the blending of statute and common law, a beautifully complex and intricate system that both draws on tradition and is adaptable. On the whole, though, common law rewards sticking to precedent. In many jurisdictions, especially in the US, lawyers live in fear of their clients suing them. In addition, few clients are fans of high-risk legal strategies. As a result, most lawyers live their lives deeply attached to the status quo, especially if they're already making comfortable livelihoods.

Large international law firms also tend to be conservative. After all, they have hundreds of partners scattered across the globe, and the safest way to keep everyone happy is by playing things safe. Smaller firms tend to follow the lead of larger firms because they see them as the leaders of the profession.

When we talked to Jil Toovey about lawyers and risk aversion, she explained how risk aversion affects a lawyer's attitude to any kind of innovation connected to new technology. Any new innovation may not work straight away. If a particular strategy doesn't work, the normal response will be to tinker and refine it. However, lawyers will simply say, 'That didn't work', and throw it out.

At the same time, Jil has run innovation workshops with lawyers which show that if you give them permission to be creative and imaginative, they thrive because they are very bright and, often, when given permission, really enjoy coming up with ideas and challenging the status quo. She claimed it was possible to get them to come up, in a couple of days, with incredibly clever answers to environmental problems and the challenge of achieving world peace. Jil said she'd done these kinds of exercises with other professionals and come out thinking, 'Is that all you've got?' However, she rarely felt that with lawyers. She concluded, 'I think a lot of them [lawyers] are inherently creative but the fear of failure or mistakes stifles them.'

In the end, lawyers are programmed to avoid risk, not get anything wrong and have absolute clarity, which makes things tricky when dealing with problems or challenges that don't have concrete answers. This makes the relationship between lawyers and marketing and business development challenging because marketing and business development don't always present concrete answers. Once again, if you run up against risk aversion in your efforts to launch a new marketing strategy, you may need to point out that risk aversion is a common trait in lawyers and ask them whether they think that this mode of thinking is blocking initiative.

Lawyers are intellectual piranhas

The nature of legal training means that lawyers tend to be intellectual piranhas: that is, they have a tendency to tear apart new ideas because they are so used to focusing on identifying risk. This means that a law firm can be a difficult place to introduce new ideas.

Jil Toovey described the inefficiency that results from living in a world populated by intellectual piranhas:

> *The problem is that you get the intellectual piranhas in a room and they are programmed to critique and find the holes in things. One person says, 'What if we offer the client a secondment option as a value-add in the tender?' and everyone else rips that idea to shreds. It goes on and on. Everyone feels great because they are so critical and they've found every possible risk. Then, the hour is up and they say, 'We'll have to meet again about this.' These kinds of meetings take place day in, day out in law firms. In the meantime, the things that you are talking about, specifically digital issues, are passing them by. A digital person may come in and suggest all these things but they say, 'But what about this? What about that?'*

Once again, the most appropriate strategy to use when you find that a room full of lawyers is tearing your idea apart is to be able to back up whatever you want to do with evidence that supports your argument.

Lawyers don't like change

Like most people, lawyers don't like change.

Ultimately, human beings do what they feel like doing, and, like any human being, most lawyers feel like doing what they did yesterday.

In his book, *Strategy and the Fat Smoker*, David Maister has pointed out that many change efforts are based on the assumption that all you have to do is explain to people that their lives could be better, convince them that the goals are worth going for, and show them how to do it. However, this assumption is patently false. If it were true, there would be no drug addicts, no alcoholics and no bad marriages. Maister cites the hypothetical example of a person who walks up to him and says, 'Look at how fabulous it would be if you were a fit, non-smoking exerciser, David!' His usual response is, 'True, but please shut up and go away.' Maister goes on to point out that the primary reason we do not work at behaviours that we know we need to improve is that the rewards (and pleasure) are in the future; the disruption, discomfort and discipline needed to get there are immediate.[27]

Lawyers, like other human beings, are not good at delayed gratification. Like everyone else, they may start self-improvement programs with good intentions, but if the program doesn't pay off immediately, or if a temptation to depart from it arises, they abandon the effort completely until the next time they pretend to get on the program.

The reality is that most people don't change until faced with a crisis.

A good example that David Maister often uses to demonstrate this point is the fat smoker who has a heart attack and suddenly gives up smoking, starts exercising and loses 20 kilograms.

The same rule applies to law firms and lawyers. More often than not, it is difficult to get a law firm to implement organisational or cultural change unless it is faced with a disaster. Once again, this is an area where you can use evidence to support your argument for change. For example, it may be effective to use examples of other firms where a change initiative was implemented successfully.

Lawyers don't like talking about marketing

As we've explained, most lawyers at firms are under constant pressure to bill hours in order to justify their presence there. While they are happy to talk to clients, especially if they can bill for that time, they can view talking to colleagues as a distraction. Discussing non-billable issues can also be viewed as a major diversion from what is important. This antisocial attitude not only makes it difficult to build a convivial workplace environment but ensures it is almost impossible to get anything done because no one has time to discuss anything, let alone make a decision.

Once again, timing can be everything when it comes down to getting key decisions made in a law firm. In this respect, it helps if every marketer and business development professional is a skilled strategist who knows exactly when to present that proposal or plan to management.

Lawyers don't like mumbo jumbo

Lawyers tend not to have much tolerance for mumbo jumbo or gobbledygook. In short, more often than not, lawyers are intolerant of sentences or phrases that say very little. This is because they have finely tuned analytical skills, and frequently use them to tear apart the logic of an argument or the terms of a contract.

Ironically, many lawyers are fond of legalese because that is the language they use every day. In addition, the lawyer monopoly on legalese helps preserve the profession's mystique. In fact, the ability to speak and write legalese is what distinguishes lawyers from other people. This produces a strange dichotomy in the legal mind. Despite their hostility to mumbo jumbo, most lawyers feel comfortable hiding behind legal expressions or phrases because doing so gives the impression that law is a special skill that only the elite few can master.

Most lawyers would regard marketing as filled with mumbo jumbo, and the terminology associated with digital technology as full of technobabble. In many ways, it is a fair criticism. For this reason, we would encourage you to try to explain any idea or plan in clear language. After all, it is a real skill to explain a complex idea clearly.

We also advise you never to assume knowledge. As a result, if you use marketing terminology, you should always explain it.

Lawyers think they are wordsmiths

Due to their fluency in legalese, most lawyers are convinced that they are highly skilled wordsmiths. Sadly, the ability to prepare an affidavit or draft a contract using legalese doesn't necessarily mean lawyers are good at using words to communicate a clear and coherent marketing message, especially to an audience made up of non-lawyers. Even when communicating with fellow lawyers, things can get very dry and dull, and even con-voluted. Anyone who has worked in a law firm will have come across the lawyer who insists on using ten-line sentences that no one else can understand.

In 2013, Bryan A. Garner, an American lawyer, lexicographer, academic and author of more than two dozen books on English usage and style, published an article titled 'Why lawyers can't write'.[28] In this piece, he announced that practising lawyers, when it comes to writing, are like 23-handicap golfers who believe that they're equal to the touring professionals. In short, they are delusional.

Garner went on to explain most lawyers suffer from something known as the Dunning-Kruger effect.

What is the Dunning-Kruger effect?

In 1999, two Cornell University psychologists

conducted a series of studies showing that unskilful or unknowledgeable people:

- often think they are quite skilful or knowledgeable
- can't recognise genuine skill in others
- uniformly fail to recognise the extremity of their own inadequacy
- can recognise and acknowledge their own previous unskillfulness only after highly effective training in the skill.

According to Garner, the incidence of Dunning-Kruger is significantly higher among transactional lawyers than it is among litigators. He explained:

This is puzzling but true. While lawyers are the most highly paid rhetoricians in the world, we're among the most inept wielders of words. Stop and think about that. The blame goes primarily to the law schools. They inundate students with poorly written, legalese-riddled opinions that read like over-the-top Marx Brothers parodies of stiffness and hyperformality.

The problem with lawyers and writing is even more extreme when they have to change gears and write something that is intended to persuade another human being (quite possibly a non-lawyer) to pick up the phone and call them. The challenge is to get lawyers to recognise that there are different styles of writing that are appropriate to different circumstances, and that clients will always be attracted to the Cyrano de Bergeracs of the legal world because their writing skills are a reflection of their communication skills.

This is obviously a sensitive topic for lawyers. For this reason, we suggest you adopt a gentle approach to educating them about writing. One effective way of educating a lawyer is to take the time to provide detailed feedback on any piece they generate that has a promotional purpose and explain exactly why you have made changes to it.

Lawyers are suspicious of people who don't understand legal concepts

Lawyers can be reluctant to work with people who don't understand legal concepts or aren't familiar with the way law firms operate.

This is because the legal frameworks that regulate society can be complicated and, in the jurisdictions where the common law intersects with statutes, the picture is even more intricate. In short, lawyers have a monopoly on the way law works and, for this reason, they think they are special. Consequently, they tend to be suspicious of working with non-lawyers because they doubt that a person who hasn't graduated from law school can understand what lawyers do.

As a marketer or business development professional working in a law firm, you will gradually find that you learn quite a bit about law from the lawyers you work with. We would also encourage you to ask questions, and demonstrate that you are interested in getting the law right and in assisting them to find the best possible way to communicate complex legal concepts to clients.

Lawyers have a duty of confidentiality to their clients

In common law jurisdictions, the duty of confidentiality between a lawyer and their client is fundamental. Confidentiality forms part of the lawyer's broader fiduciary duty to their clients and underpins the concept of legal professional privilege. In many ways, the confidential relationship between lawyers and clients is similar to doctor-patient confidentiality.

The reason behind the duty of confidentiality is to maintain full and frank disclosure between a lawyer and their client.

In practice, the duty of confidentiality means that a lawyer must keep information about a client's affairs strictly confidential. This information must not be used for the benefit of persons not authorised by the client. The consequences of breaching the duty can be extremely serious.

It is important to realise that the issue of confidentiality feeds into the broader relationship that lawyers build with their clients, often over many years. The key ingredient in any long-term relationship between lawyers and their clients is trust and any lawyer will be reluctant to put that relationship in jeopardy.

The duty of confidentiality can cause tension between marketers and lawyers. This is because, on one hand, marketers are always keen to use lawyer success stories to sell both the individual lawyer and the firm to prospective clients. On the other hand, lawyers are reluctant to do anything that could lead them to breach their duty of confidentiality.

So, we would advise that, if you want to use client names, examples or case studies in any marketing materials, you should:

- show you are aware of lawyer-client confidentiality issues
- discuss the possibility of using a client name, matter example or case study with the lawyer you are working with
- suggest that the lawyer might like to talk about the possibility of using a client name, matter example or case study with the client. It may turn out that the client, especially if they value the lawyer's professional skills, doesn't have any objections to their name or matter being used as an example on a website or in marketing collateral
- offer the relevant client the opportunity to review any marketing material before it is published.

In the end, as a marketer or business development professional, it is important to show that you not only respect the relationship between lawyers and clients but understand it, especially when it comes to confidentiality.

You may even find that if a client has waived confidentiality and has given a lawyer permission to use a particular case or transaction as a matter example in marketing material or in a media opportunity, the lawyer may still be reluctant to discuss the matter in any depth. In these cases, it may be necessary to talk the lawyer through the issues and help them move beyond their deeply ingrained concerns about confidentiality so they can use the opportunity to demonstrate their skills and talents as a lawyer to prospective clients.

Lawyers often struggle when it comes to implementation

Most change initiatives in law firms fail.

This means that, even if an idea (such as a plan to embark on a digital marketing strategy) attracts support, it never gets off the ground. This is especially true in smaller firms that don't have marketing teams, and where the focus is on billable hours and managing partners run practices alongside their management responsibilities.

In our experience, and from talking to people working in the industry, it makes sense to keep projects small and realistic, especially if you're working in a small firm. Alternatively, you may find it more effective to break larger projects into stages.

Lawyers don't like to ask for help

Another trait that we've noticed in lawyers is that, when it comes to non-legal activities such as marketing and business development, they don't always like asking for help.

As we've already mentioned, most lawyers tend to be high achievers. In addition, many are perfectionists. This means that not only are they good at what they do but they take pride in the quality of their professional work. As we've pointed out, the competitive atmosphere in a law firm means that most lawyers are reluctant to admit that anyone can offer them support – particularly non-lawyers.

Nevertheless, lawyers, like the rest of us, are human and very few are brilliant at every task involved in being a legal professional.

For example, lawyers think and analyse in a specific way. In addition, they write in a specific way. If a lawyer spends most of their day drafting legal documents, it is understandable that their writing style becomes shaped by the requirements and objectives of those documents. For many lawyers, this becomes a professional hazard because it means they struggle to change gears when it comes to adopting different styles of writing, such as article writing, which has become an important part of law firm content marketing. This isn't because they lack a talent for writing. Rather, it is because they have been living in a writing straightjacket in order to do their job.

In many cases, the lawyer will be aware of this problem even if they don't talk about it openly. Even more significantly, their professional pride and perfectionist tendencies tend to prevent them from understanding that marketing professionals are highly trained professionals who can do a better job when it comes to producing marketing and business development material.

Another example of where a lawyer may be reluctant to ask for help or support is when it comes to general business development and marketing activities. As we've pointed out, a lot of lawyers, especially those we've identified as dinosaurs and laser beams, struggle with the idea of marketing. If you get them to open up, they may even say things like, 'How I loathe the business of law! It's driving me out of the profession.' On the one hand, this kind of statement is an understandable expression of frustration for someone who thought they were entering a profession but has discovered they also need to operate like a businessperson. On the other hand, it presents as the perfect opportunity for a marketing professional to add value to the business of law. This is because the kind of thinking that is involved in practising as a lawyer is very different from the kind of thinking you need to do in order to sell your services to prospective clients.

As a result, ideally, as a marketer and business development professional, you should be educating the lawyers in your firm about marketing concepts and ideas. In addition, you should encourage your lawyers to step out of their comfort zone, specifically the traditional, narrow, legal mode of thinking, and help them to adopt more creative and entrepreneurial modes of analysis.

Nevertheless, in most firms, you will probably have to take a gentle approach to 'education'. You need to be both humble and patient. You may need to break down the 'education process' into a number of steps such as:

Step 1: Win the trust and respect of the lawyers in your firm by not only producing high-quality work but making an effort to understand what lawyers do. For example, try to attend team meetings and ask questions when appropriate.

Step 2: Introduce them to marketing and business development ideas and concepts slowly. This can be as simple as delivering a presentation, at an event like a team offsite or a firm strategy day, on how your team can bring value to the table.

Step 3: Identify the lawyers in your firm who are interested in marketing and business development and ensure they become your allies.

Step 4: If possible, set up a pilot project with a team within the firm that is receptive to marketing and business development concepts and use these projects as examples of successful strategies. You can then use these successful examples to launch firm-wide marketing campaigns.

Your ultimate goal should be to ensure that as many lawyers as possible in your firm have an understanding of the concepts behind marketing and business development, as well as appreciate its practical value to the firm in terms of pushing prospective clients through the sales-conversion funnel.

Lawyers appreciate high-quality work (especially if they think it may lead to a large number of clients walking through the door)

Although all the traits mentioned above make it difficult to collaborate with lawyers, working with them can also be rewarding.

First, although marketing a law firm is a major challenge, if you manage to do it well or come up with something different, it is very satisfying.

Second, lawyers tend to be clever, and it is always interesting working with clever people who can give you high-quality feedback that improves the quality of the end product. Occasionally, lawyers get interested in a marketing project and really sink their teeth into it. These are the moments when the magic happens.

6: HOW LAWYERS SEE MARKETING

Marketing is a very different discipline from law because it is both a science and an art.

While law is about identifying the issues and applying the legal principles in order to come up with a solution, marketing attracts people who have entrepreneurial tendencies, and like to build and design projects from scratch without knowing for certain whether they will work. While there are theories behind marketing and business development strategies, there is always an element of trial and error.

Furthermore, a particular marketing campaign may need to be tweaked several times before it reaps rewards.

As a marketer, you would be aware that there are many textbooks devoted to marketing strategy – the art of making it all work. These tomes include powerful theories such as the Ansoff Matrix, the Consumer Decision-Making Process, Porter's Five Forces, and Maslow's Hierarchy of Needs, which are designed to solve business problems and improve marketing strategies.

And if a large company is going to invest millions of

dollars in a new global strategy or an innovative product, the research and development side of marketing is very important. Each year, billions of dollars are spent on this worldwide.

At its heart, marketing is developing a deep understanding of markets. Working out what people *need and want*, then satisfying those needs and wants better than your competitors.

So, despite its soft reputation, marketing is a rigorous, numbers-based science that informs a creative process, and that businesses around the globe rely on to make super profits. It would be fair to say, based on our research, that marketing, in its truest sense, is largely misunderstood by lawyers. Few lawyers realise that marketing is statistically based and scientific in its approach, especially on the marketing research side of the equation.

You could be excused for thinking that the marketing we see in law firms is evidence that the discipline has been hijacked and a less sophisticated form of it put in its place. This type of marketing fails to tap into the theories and methodology in any kind of meaningful way. In fact, law firms could be even more profitable if they applied real marketing theories in their business planning.

We believe that the major challenge for marketers and business development professionals is to ensure that the lawyers they work with see the legal profession as a business.

Next, marketers need to educate lawyers about marketing. More specifically, they need to explain to lawyers that marketing isn't just a matter of applying a formula. Rather, it is a combination of using a methodology to undertake research to analyse their market, and then to develop strategies to tap into that market. The former ideally involves extensive research, and the latter involves combining well-established marketing theories with creative thinking and applying it.

The trouble with the word 'marketing'

Jil Toovey identified one of the primary reasons behind the tension between lawyers and marketers when she told us:

> *I think the word 'marketing' is a real problem. I think it sounds shallow and tinny. Lawyers and marketers have a different focus … Marketers would say that we are looking at opportunities and possibilities, global trends and emerging technologies. Whereas lawyers would say that we are looking at billable hours, getting things right and reducing risk.*

Jil went on to explain that she thinks lawyers see marketers as an inferior professional tribe that they don't understand. To the average lawyer, they seem vague, comfortable with mistakes and lacking rigour. In addition, marketers don't appreciate typical lawyer qualities, such as a respect for tradition, heathy conservatism and accuracy.

Lawyers' discomfort with marketing may also have its

origins in the traditional restrictions that were placed on the advertising of legal services. However, as advertising bans have been lifted around the world and as we move to a more uniform approach, marketing and business development have become increasingly important in the lives of both law firms and lawyers. With the digital revolution, the marketing of legal services has become an even more important part of law firm life. And, in some ways, the growth of digital technology has forced law firms to grapple with more sophisticated forms of marketing. To be successful with digital advertising, law firms need to know their target markets and segment them. This is a boon for marketing types who have longed to get serious about marketing in law firms.

Most large law firms created marketing departments out of necessity rather than passion. After all, in the 1980s, when the larger firms began to add marketing departments, the profession was transforming. Firms didn't want to be left behind, so they added marketing departments, sometimes very half-heartedly, just in case there was something in what they saw as the 'sordid science of marketing'.

There are still lawyers who remember the good old days before marketing and business development departments in law firms. As a result, they feel a certain nostalgia for the time when work came in solely via contacts and referrals because business development and marketing were not needed.

A lot of lawyers find the concept of 'digital marketing'

even more problematic than 'marketing'. After all, it involves narcissistic activities such as blog posting and publicising oneself through social media. Even if lawyers are egocentric, they don't necessarily enjoy hawking their wares in cyberspace. In addition, many lawyers, especially older lawyers, simply don't understand digital marketing. Both the concepts and language make them uncomfortable.

Marketers and lawyers speak different languages

Through our own experiences of working with lawyers and marketers, one of the most common themes that emerges is the 'cultural' gap that exists between lawyers and marketers.

This is reflected in a range of areas, from the way people working in marketing and advertising think, dress and behave, to their use of language, and even extends to the way they interact with their colleagues.

After all, stories of lawyers being completely baffled by an advertising executive arriving on a motorbike, and dressed in a leather jacket, to discuss the mysteries of the firm's branding are legendary. You can see the lawyers sitting round the table shuddering when he tells them, 'And the splash of ultramarine in the logo symbolises innovation.'

Lawyers also often feel uneasy when working with people who don't understand legal concepts, which is understandable. Anyone who has worked in a communications role in a law firm has probably heard the words, 'You've changed the meaning of my article.'

Lawyers often use specific terms or nuanced language because they are a crucial part of a legal concept. Sometimes using a simpler word or term is inappropriate because it has a different legal meaning. As a result, it is always a good idea to consult the lawyer you work with before you change the terminology in their article. This is not only a courtesy but shows you understand the specific and unique way lawyers use language.

At the same time, most communications professionals working in law firms will recall feeling slightly desperate when a dry and dull article full of impenetrable legalese, even though it was intended for non-lawyers, has landed on their desk. In addition, most communications managers struggle to get the lawyers at their firms to write articles that are:

- interesting
- able to be understood by a non-lawyer
- well written.

In the end, it is a balancing exercise – you need to encourage your lawyers to use clear and simple language while ensuring that you don't twist the legal meaning with insensitive editing. Our rule is always, 'If in doubt, check with the lawyer who wrote the article.'

Marketers and lawyers value different skill sets

When you think about it, the skills and capabilities that are valued in a chief marketing officer (CMO) are very different from those that are valued in a senior lawyer, especially a senior lawyer seen as having management potential.

All the most recent literature agrees that in a CMO, you are looking for a person who has an independent and entrepreneurial attitude but can work closely with other departments.[29]

A CMO should be a risk taker, be willing to make decisions, have problem-solving ability, be an agent for change and be focused on achieving results. In addition, they should have cross-industry experience, a digital focus and a knowledge of operations. Finally, they need to have the ability to build a working environment that encourages the exploration of ideas.

While some of these qualities overlap with the qualities found in lawyers, you can see that attributes such as being a 'risk taker' and 'agent for change' don't align at all with the skills and capabilities that lawyers value.

In addition, a CMO should act as the visionary for the future of the company, build adaptive marketing capabilities and win the war for marketing talent. Ideally, they should include the client's perspective in business decisions affecting any client 'touch point' with the firm.

The trouble with this is that most CMOs are non-lawyers, which makes it hard for them to understand what clients want and need. Even if they do understand the clients and can bring a fresh perspective, it is hard for them to convince the lawyers (who deal with their clients on a daily basis) that they know what they are talking about.

In marketing, innovation is critical. The reality is that imaginative ideas for business strategies exist in many places within a company. Senior management should identify and encourage fresh ideas from three generally under-represented groups:

1. employees with youthful or diverse perspectives
2. employees far removed from company headquarters
3. employees new to the industry.

These groups' inputs are valuable because they can challenge company orthodoxy and stimulate new ideas.

The trouble is that most lawyers loathe the word 'innovation', and most law firms are structured in a way that disempowers younger employees and non-lawyers.

Lawyers don't understand the work that marketers and business development professionals undertake

There is little doubt that lawyers don't have a clear idea of what marketers and business development professionals actually do.

This lack of understanding occurs partly because the role of a marketer or business development professional can be very diverse. It can involve anything from managing a website revamp, designing a business plan for the entire firm, developing a branding strategy, preparing a tender response, drafting copy for a brochure or managing a social media campaign, to developing a content marketing strategy.

In larger firms, the role of a marketer or business development professional may be very specific. In smaller firms, the role may be much more general and cover a broader range of areas. This can be a problem because what is expected of marketers and business development professionals varies greatly from firm to firm.

What is expected of the marketing and business development roles in law firms?

Whether in a more traditional marketing and business development team or a more contemporary national client and market growth team, the baseline expectations of marketing and business development roles are similar across most traditional firms and tend to fit into three broad categories:

1. coordinator
2. manager
3. director.

You may find it necessary to explain to the lawyers in your firm exactly what you do, and the descriptions below will help.

Coordinator

In this type of entry-level role, you will be expected to provide support for marketing and business development activities, rather than driving results. Coordinators need to have good technical skills in writing, editing, PowerPoint and web publishing, and be able to assist with press releases, capability statements, pitch books and tenders. But they are not responsible for developing strategy, the outcome of tenders or managing budgets. 'Previous law firm experience a plus' is how these jobs are often advertised, and this is code for 'You need to understand our culture and mode of operation, know our systems and have a thick skin.'

Manager

At a manager level, you will be expected to make things happen. You will need to be able to work closely with partners to support practice areas, and also to develop and execute campaigns. You will also need to be able to support the growth of business development skills among lawyers, as well as formulate strategy for responses to clients in the form of tenders and capability statements. You will need to be able to work with graphic designers, manage external consultants, and direct work flow internally and externally. Most importantly, you will need to be able to manage a budget.

Director

Once you reach director level, you will need the experience and skills to bring everything together. As a director, you will work closely with the partners and direct all the firm's marketing, communications, events and business development resources, so that they achieve the firm's overarching strategic goals.

In addition, it is the strength of vision of the director of a marketing and business development team in a law firm that determines whether a marketing strategy will be successful. A director will also need the support of management to implement their marketing strategy. Much like the C-Suite roles we discussed earlier, directors really need to have a 'seat at the table' to be effective.

Other marketing and business development roles

Due to the impact of the digital revolution and associated technological change, there are an increasing number of new marketing and business development roles in law firms that reflect how firms are transforming, as well as responding to the needs and expectations of their clients. These roles include: digital specialist, client experience advisor, executive director of sales, business development executive, event specialist, public relations and communications specialist, pursuit and bids manager, client experience and analytics manager, bid delivery coordinator, graphic designer and pitch manager (to name just a few).

In terms of baseline expectations for these roles, they can vary but tend to fall into the 'manager' or 'coordinator' categories of authority and responsibility outlined above.

The importance of educating lawyers about marketing

As a marketer or business development professional, you should educate your lawyers about marketing, especially those lawyers in management positions. This is a key activity which we discussed in Chapters 5 and 6, which is worth reiterating.

In many cases, you will find lawyers have no idea that there is a difference between sales, marketing and business development.

In addition, you need to explain that marketing is a sophisticated mode of research and analysis that draws on a range of disciplines, including psychology, sociology, economics and management.

Most importantly, this educating process isn't about telling lawyers what to do. Rather, it is a matter of building a bridge between lawyers and marketers, so they understand each other better and can work together to develop more effective marketing strategies.

7: A FEW CONCLUDING WORDS

We hope this journey through the world of law firms has given you an understanding of the structure and culture of law firms, as well as some insight into the way lawyers think and operate.

Even more importantly, we hope we've given you some practical strategies that you can use to build better relationships with the lawyers in your firm.

In the end, we believe that the key to law firms developing marketing strategies that are going to have a real impact is narrowing the gap between lawyers and marketers via both communication and education.

Marketers and business development professionals need to focus on ensuring their lawyers develop a more sophisticated understanding of marketing. You need to show them that marketing isn't just about making documents look pretty. Instead, it is a research-based discipline that employs both analytical thinking and creativity. This process involves convincing lawyers that if they are going to be able to adapt to the technological transformation sweeping the legal services industry, they need to think not only analytically and strategically but creatively.

If you are a marketer or business development professional working in a law firm, we would like to encourage you to fight for 'a seat at the table' because we believe your skills and insights can help lawyers adapt to the digital era.

Remember: it's all about building a better relationship with the lawyers in your firm so you can work closely together to create effective marketing and business development strategies.

ACKNOWLEDGEMENTS

During the process of investigating the causes of the gap between lawyers and marketers in law firms, we talked to quite a few lawyers and marketers, as well as experts in leadership and change management.

We would like to thank Gerry Riskin for both his enthusiasm and support for this project, as well as agreeing to write the Foreword.

Special thanks must go to Avril Henry and Jil Toovey for their insights and invaluable contributions to this book.

During the course of researching and writing this book, we appreciated the opportunity to talk to Charles Ashton, Andrew Barnes, Tony Bleasdale, Michael Bradley, Jack Buchanan, Gail Christopher, Stuart Clark, Tony Giurissevich, Ray Hartley, Veronica Hartley, Ursula Hogben, David Jones, David Kearney, Nicki Hauser, Anthony Lieu, Daniel Lipman Lowbeer, Elena Lonergan, Warwick McLean, Kersten Norlin, Murray Prior, Sue-Ella Prodonovich, Jeremy Richman, Daniel Rod, Steve Sampson, Chad Sluss, Amber Spiby, Kenneth Stanton, Freeda

Stevenson, Richard Travers, Susan Warda and Katherine Webster. Either through formal or informal discussions, each of these people helped test our ideas about how the structure and culture of law firms, as well as the different ways lawyers and marketers think, shape the relationship between lawyers and marketers. These conversations also gave us plenty of food for thought. For that, we are incredibly grateful and thank them all profusely for being so generous with their time. However, they are in no way responsible for the views expressed in this book or any errors. Those are ours and ours alone.

Editors always play a crucial role in the emergence of any book from an idea into something with pages and a cover. For this reason, we would like to express our appreciation for the skills and talent of our editors, Sarina Rowell and Lilla Wendoloski.

Finally, we would like to acknowledge the assistance and support of Carroll & O'Dea Lawyers.

Would you like to find out more about how to build bridges between fee earners and fee burners in your firm?

Visit our website:
www.marketersguidetolawfirms.com

NOTES AND REFERENCES

[1] Consultancy.uk, 'Employees in professional services critical of business development teams', 7 September 2017 <https://www.consultancy.uk/news/13947/employees-in-professional-services-critical-of-business-development-teams>.

[2] Australasian Legal Practice Management Association and Julian Midwinter & Associates, *Winning Work in a Digital World: Benchmarking Marketing & Business Development in Australasian Law Firms* (2015).

[3] Miriam Rozen, 'Marketing professionals play more significant role at law firms, survey results show', *The American Lawyer*, 10 April 2018

<https://www.law.com/americanlawyer/2018/04/10/marketing-professionals-play-more-significant-role-at-law-firms-survey-results-show>.

[4] National Organization of Bar Counsel, 'Alternative business structures: frequently asked questions' <https://nobc.org/resources/Documents/State%20Disciplinary%20Flowcharts/Alternate.Business.Structures.FAQ.Final.pdf>.

[5] Samantha Steer, 'ABS models rise in the UK', Forum Magazine, 27 September 2017 <https://blogs.thomsonreuters.com/answerson/abs-models-rise-in-the-uk>.

[6] Law Council of Australia, *National Attrition and Re-engagement Study (NARS)* Report <https://www.lawcouncil.asn.au/policy-agenda/advancing-the-profession/equal-opportunities-in-the-law/national-report-on-attrition-and-re-engagement>.

[7] Julie I. Fershtman, 'Lawyer bullies: what to do about it', ABA News, November 2014 <https://www.americanbar.org/news/abanews/publications/youraba/2014/november-2014/bullying-by-and-of-lawyers>.

[8] Jane Lee, 'Bullying judges breed stressful system: Kirby', *The Age*, 22 February 2013 <https://www.theage.com.au/national/victoria/bullying-judges-breed-stress-ful-system-kirby-20130221-2eudp.html>.

[9] 'Out of the darkness: overcoming depression among lawyers', *ABA News*, March

2015 <https://www.americanbar.org/groups/gpsolo/publications/gp_solo/2015/ march-april/out_the_darkness_overcoming_depression_among_lawyers>.

[10] Tyger Latham, 'The depressed lawyer: why are so many lawyers so unhappy?', *Psychology Today*, 2 May 2011 <https://www.psychologytoday.com/us/blog/ therapy-matters/201105/the-depressed-lawyer>.

[11] Aidan Macnab, 'High-pressure law jobs linked to depression', *Canadian Lawyer*, 26 October 2017 <http://www.canadianlawyermag.com/legalfeeds/ high-pressure-law-jobs-linked-to-depression-14835/>.

[12] Karen Jackson, 'Stress and the legal profession', *The Law Society News*, 19 May 2016 <http://www.lawsociety.org.uk/news/blog/stress-and-the-legal-profession>.

[13] Beyond Blue, 'Annual Professions Survey: Research Summary', April 2007 <http://www.judicialcollege.vic.edu.au/sites/default/files/2007%20-%20 Beyond%20Blue%20-%20Annual%20Professions%20Survey.pdf>.

[14] Norman Kelk et al, *Courting the Blues: Attitudes Towards Depression in Australian Law Students and Lawyers*, Brain & Mind Research Institute Monograph 2009-1, University of Sydney <https://cald.asn.au/wp-content/uploads/2017/11/ BMRI-Report-Courting-the-BluesLaw-Report-Website-version-4-May-091.pdf>.

[15] Peter Gregory, 'Lawyers depressed and stressed, says survey', *The Sydney Morning Herald*, 18 September 2008 <http://www.smh.com.au/national/lawyers-depressed-and-stressed-says-survey-20080918-4iym.html>.

[16] Sharon Medlow, Norm Kelk and Ian Hickie, 'Depression and the law: experiences of Australian barristers and solicitors' (2011) 33 *Sydney Law Review* 771 <http://www.austlii.edu.au/cgi-bin/viewdoc/au/journals/SydLawRw/2011/31.html?context=1;query=%22Depression%20and%20the%20law%22;mask_path=au/ journals/SydLawRw>.

[17] 'Young lawyer outs depression that is endemic in the legal profession', *Australian Financial Review,* 29 September 2015 <http://www.afr.com/lifestyle/health/ mens-health/young-lawyer-outs-depression-that-is-endemic-in-legal-profession-20150927-gjw3bu>.

[18] Aidan Macnab, 'High-pressure law jobs linked to depression', *Canadian Lawyer*, 26 October 2017 <http://www.canadianlawyermag.com/legalfeeds/ high-pressure-law-jobs-linked-to-depression-14835>; Michelle McQuigge, 'Lawyers who excel in their work more likely to suffer depression: study', *The Canadian Press,* 22 October 2017 <https://globalnews.ca/news/3818613/ lawyers-mental-health-depression-increases-with-success>.

[19] This discussion of generational issues in law firms is based on American

Management Association, 'Leading the four generations at work' <http://www.amanet.org/training/articles/Leading-the-Four-Generations-at-Work.aspx> and our interview with Avril Henry.

[20] The College of Law, 'Encouraging gender diversity in the legal profession', 13 March 2014 <https://www.collaw.edu.au/news/2016/11/14/encouraging-gender-diversity-in-the-legal-profession>.

[21] Law Council of Australia, *National Attrition and Re-engagement Study (NARS)* Report <https://www.lawcouncil.asn.au/policy-agenda/advancing-the-profession/equal-opportunities-in-the-law/national-report-on-attrition-and-re-engagement>.

[22] Solicitors Regulation Authority, 'How diverse are law firms?' August 2017 <http://www.sra.org.uk/solicitors/diversity-toolkit/diverse-law-firms.page>.

[23] American Bar Association, Commission on Women in the Profession, *A Current Glance at Women in the Law: January 2017* (2017) <https://www.americanbar.org/content/dam/aba/marketing/women/current_glance_statistics_january2017.authcheckdam.pdf>.

[24] Gabriela Tavella and Gordon Parker, 'How to tell if you're really "burnt out"', *The Sydney Morning Herald*, 15 May 2018 <https://www.smh.com.au/lifestyle/health-and-wellness/how-to-tell-if-you-re-really-burnt-out-20180514-p4zf5h.html>.

[25] 'Down by law, with the black dog', *The Sydney Morning Herald*, 7 September 2006 <https://www.smh.com.au/national/down-by-law-with-the-black-dog-20060907-gdoc8n.html>.

[26] 'Why do barristers wear black robes?' (2005) 1 *Western Australian Bar Association Review* 29.

[27] David Maister, *Strategy and the Fat Smoker: Doing What's Obvious But Not Easy* (Spangle Press, 2008).

[28] Bryan A. Garner, 'Why lawyers can't write', *ABA Journal*, March 2013 <http://www.abajournal.com/magazine/article/why_lawyers_cant_write>.

[29] Shelly Kramer, 'The modern CMO: adaptable, innovative, agile', *Futurum*, 8 August 2016 <https://www.futurum.xyz/the-modern-cmo-adaptable-innovative-agile>; Daniel Newman, 'Personality traits of an exceptionally strong CMO', *Forbes*, 27 December 2016 <https://www.forbes.com/sites/daniel-newman/2016/12/27/personality-traits-of-an-exceptionally-strong-cmo/#5a-ecd64f3c34>; David Clarke, 'The nine traits of highly effective CMOs', *strategy+business*, 1 June 2017 <https://www.strategy-business.com/blog/The-Nine-Traits-of-Highly-Effective-CMOs?gko=c45b2>.

www.ingramcontent.com/pod-product-compliance
Lightning Source LLC
Chambersburg PA
CBHW031951190326
41519CB00007B/755